MEDITATION

*Transforming our lives for the encounter
with Christ*

Jörgen Smit

Translated by Anna R. Meuss and Johanna Collis

Sophia Books

Sophia Books
Hillside House, The Square
Forest Row, E. Sussex
RH18 5ES

www.rudolfsteinerpress.com

Published by Sophia Books 1996
An imprint of Rudolf Steiner Press

First English edition by Rudolf Steiner Press 1991
Revised second edition 1996
Reprinted 2007

Originally published in German under the title *Meditation und Christus-Erfahrung. Wege zur Verwandlung des eigenen Lebens* by Verlag Freies Geistesleben, Stuttgart, in 1990

A catalogue record for this book is available from the British Library

ISBN 978 185584 149 9

Cover by Andrew Morgan
Typeset by DP Photosetting, Aylesbury, Bucks.
Printed and bound in Great Britain by 4edge Limited, Essex

Contents

First Steps

There is a general tendency today, among those who look to meditation as a way of broadening consciousness, to turn away from the ideas and opinions of our modern age—ideas that are largely determined by the way in which scientists see the world—and seek to achieve quite different levels of consciousness, which frequently have no connection with the scientific way of thinking.

In anthroposophy, on the other hand, the meditative path to knowledge firmly takes everyday consciousness as its starting point and first of all sets out to explore its boundaries. It is not a matter of simply giving up the old for something new, but rather of broadening the conscious experience that we have gained in an age when science largely determines our views. This is not done by speculation and theory, but by developing new faculties, faculties that we already have, but which are dormant.

The point is, then, to make use of a potential for growth and development that already exists, and not fill the mind with alien notions or seek to dress it up in foreign garb. We must learn to see where such potential lies, for the seeds are already there and can be made to grow well beyond the boundaries of our present conscious experience.

The potential we have for opening up consciousness is anything but small; in fact it is vast. We have to start small, however.

The following analogy will give a clearer picture of the steps that can be taken to broaden our consciousness.

Higher level of consciousness
|
Everyday level of consciousness
|
Sleep level of consciousness

In the middle is our everyday consciousness. Below it is the level of consciousness we have in sleep (the level of dream consciousness is ignored for present purposes). Sleep here means deep, dreamless sleep, with consciousness reduced to a point where it has no content. Sleep-walkers will of course be active even at this level, but they are unconscious of this. This is a level where we have profound and total darkness.

We need to go to this level of consciousness night after night for the health of our waking daytime consciousness, but we are of course unable to do any of the things in deep sleep that we are able to do when awake.

Above the waking level is a higher level of consciousness. It is exactly as far above the waking level as the deep sleep level is below it. Just as we are able to look down from waking consciousness to the level of sleep consciousness, where we know nothing of what we are doing or what goes on around us, so we are able to look down from the level of higher consciousness—once we have fully achieved it—to our everyday consciousness. This everyday level does not lose significance when we achieve higher consciousness, just as our sleep consciousness does not lose significance because we also have waking consciousness.

When we look down from higher consciousness to our waking consciousness, everything we do at that level will appear to us the way sleep-walking does when seen from the waking state.

From the point of view of our higher consciousness, we really have no idea as to what is really going on when we are in the waking state. We do the oddest things, yet we simply do not know what we are doing.

A comparison between everyday consciousness and sleep consciousness reveals the specific nature of the former. Its contents are always based on what we see, hear, touch, taste and smell; we form ideas, and on the basis of these also our memories. Initially, this level of consciousness contains nothing but what we have perceived with the senses, and our memories of such perceptions. When we are asleep, all those sensory perceptions vanish, as do our memories.

The question arises whether it will be possible to go above the waking level, so that our consciousness, while remaining fully awake, can have a content that does not depend on what we have perceived with the senses, or on ideas and memories derived from this. Would it be possible to develop an inner faculty that is so powerful in its own inherent activity that it maintains itself while we are in full waking consciousness, but without having to rely on anything perceived with the senses?

For the moment, the question has to remain open, for it may well be that such a thing is not possible. Only observation and experiment can show whether such a power, or at least whether the potential, the germinating point, exists.

One such germinating point is one that every human individual can discover for himself. It is not yet at the level of that special faculty of higher consciousness, but it is related to it. We may call it the 'inner observer'.

Every adult—with few exceptions—has this inner observer, who notes everything we do, think, feel or want, and asks: What are you doing? What is going on?

It can be extremely frustrating to be aware of the inner observer at this first stage, where it is merely a focal point. Some people are bound to think that we should be much better off without it, for if one has such an observer watching all the time, spontaneity will no longer be possible. We are bound to be inhibited from opening up spontaneously in an encounter with others if we are conscious of an observer who keeps watching everything as if it were a play performed on a stage, and who makes positive or negative comments.

But this focus of self-observation—highly frustrating when all it appears to do is to inhibit spontaneous activity—also holds the potential for further development, and in that case will prove to be anything but inhibiting. We can enter into this focal point with our whole being and simply let our usual attitude rest—not all day long, but perhaps for five or ten minutes.

Then the germinal point that exists in everyday consciousness can begin to grow, and its effect will now be entirely different. A new flower can begin to unfold: stillness—undisturbed by everyday life. This is something entirely new coming into being: a new world can come to flower. The anthroposophical path of meditation can be entered upon when this potential for inner development opens up.

Different elements of this process will be described below.

The Rose Cross Meditation

A basic meditation described in considerable detail by Rudolf Steiner in his *Occult Science: An Outline* (the chapter on 'Knowledge of Higher Worlds. Concerning Initiation') is the 'Rose Cross Meditation'. It may serve as a starting point, with further steps in the meditative path of anthroposophy following on from it.

To begin with, it is important to realize that the meditation has four stages. These need not be mastered all at once. We can start at the first stage—which has its own intrinsic value—and then progress to the second, and so on, feeling in no way compelled to master all four at once.

In the first stage, the Rose Cross Meditation is developed in thought and feeling, entirely at the level of everyday consciousness. This stage is an essential preliminary for the actual image-based meditation. If we omit it, the whole meditation loses its power.

It starts with a simple comparison.

Imagine a plant growing in the garden—consider the roots that anchor it in the ground and serve as a means of taking up nourishment, the stem that raises it above ground level, the green leaves in which light is assimilated and, finally, the flower. Next, bring to mind that the plant remains in one and the same place all its life. Everything that develops in the plant is unreservedly and harmoniously integrated in the whole of the universe. There is not the slightest opposition or resistance to the environment; everything is in perfect harmony.

Consider now a human being. It is immediately obvious that people have much greater potential than plants, because they are able to move about in space and do not have to remain in one place all their lives. They move freely—not only physically all over the globe, but also in mind and spirit—creating new things that did not exist before. In everything they are, human beings go far beyond what may be regarded as essential plant nature.

At the same time, however, they have an element in them that goes equally far below plant nature. Their freedom to act also gives rise to drives and passions that have destructive properties—hatred, envy, betrayal, lies, even murder. These cause destruction not only outside but also inside the individual, ultimately perhaps even leading to suicide.

Human potential thus extends both far above and far below that of plants. People are able to act in freedom but are also able to descend to the level of drives and passions and destroy the whole earth, including their own existence.

The difference between human beings and plants is also evident in the red blood of the one and the green sap of the other. Try to enter into the experience of these qualities—blissful harmony in the green of plants and a serious mood in the red of the blood.

What does 'serious' mean in this context? It means that the blood holds the potential for both rising above and falling below the essentially human level. Thus an individual may be faced with a major decision; something tremendous may be the outcome, or things may go completely wrong. That is the 'serious' mood that may also be called the 'decision-making mood'; it differs greatly from the mood we experience in the green of plants. Everything is fixed where plants are concerned; human beings, on the other hand, may develop in one direction or in an entirely different one. The decision is still open.

We can begin, for example, to work on our drives and passions. These are not base in principle but are objective powers within us; it all depends on the context in which they are brought to bear. The powers as such are not base, but there is this aspect in them which emerges when the destructive element comes in. We can discover the base aspect of our own drives and passions and see how all this really leads to death and destruction. The death-bringing quality can be distinctly felt, and we can then come to feel that anything that is base in our drives and passions may die—not the drives and passions as such, but anything that is base in them; this has death in it, and we can let it die. Here we have a precondition for higher human development, for when those base elements die, the nature of the blood changes and it becomes the expression of a purified inner life.

Having developed this sentient inner image in the process of building up the Rose Cross Meditation, return in your mind to the plant kingdom and call up the image of a rose. The red petals of the flower show the same balanced harmony as that seen in the green of the leaves.

We consciously choose a red rose as an image representing the blood that has been purified, with base drives and passions removed. This can only be achieved, however, if we let anything that is base in our drives and passions go through death within our inner life.

The next step is to choose a symbol for the process of dying—a black cross, the image of death. The cross is the image representing anything in our drives and passions that leads to destruction, disharmony and death. Everything that thus holds death within it is condensed into the image of the black cross. Then let a circle of seven red roses come radiantly into flower on the cross, at the place where the two black bars that make up the cross intersect.

Everything that has been described so far is the first stage of the Rose Cross Meditation. We take something from everyday life as we compare plant and human being, but we choose it and put it together consciously, and an image arises in the process.

The image may be weak or powerful, depending on how strong our thoughts are as we build up the picture. The intensity of the image will also be enhanced by the feelings that go with our thoughts. If we limit the comparison between plant and human being to our thoughts and do not enter into it with feeling, the image will be cold and pale. It will grow all the more intense the more intensely we enter into the image we are building up in our thoughts. Each of the steps described above must be built up in thought and entered into with feeling in full conscious awareness: the green of the plant and the harmony between plant and environment, the red of the human blood and the potential to ascend to higher things or go down into the destructive elements in our drives, the 'serious' mood in facing decision, and so on. The thought that higher development can be achieved by taking the path that goes through death will then give rise to a feeling of happiness, and the image we have built up will be richly endowed with deep feeling.

In the second stage of the Rose Cross Meditation we allow ourselves to become utterly immersed in the image we have built up. We become totally absorbed in the image of the black cross with seven radiant red roses breaking into flower at the centre of it. Now all thoughts and reflections fall away— they were part of the first stage. The effort put into building up the image in our thoughts now creates intensity of feeling as we meditate on the Rose Cross.

If the thought effort has not been adequate, the image that arises at this second stage will lack intensity. It is obvious, therefore, that the first stage is an essential part. First the image is built up in thought, and this is followed by the actual meditation on the image where we develop a profound inner response to it.

Some people will always have the image appearing in clear, bright colours, sometimes so much so that it seems more powerful than anything seen with the physical eye. Others may find that the image is only a faint one and when the roses finally appear they are grey rather than red.

What matters, however, is the inner effort that has been made; the intensity of the image is much less important. To meditate on an image built up in this way calls for additional inner powers that we do not need for sensory perception. When we look at an outer object or call up a visual memory, this happens as if of its own accord; we do not have to do anything special. Meditation on an image, on the other hand, means that nothing is given or motivated from either outside or inside; the image has to be created out of powers that are entirely our own.

The image may also appear to be very far away, so that one wants to get closer to it. A new quality enters in if we succeed in not merely having the picture before us, so that we look at it, but in actually living within it. Then there is no longer the duality of onlooker and the thing looked on; the whole becomes a single process that we experience and to which we inwardly respond. The second stage of the Rose Cross meditation has been reached.

We may well ask why there should be seven roses coming into flower on the black cross. All that matters, surely, is to enter into the dying process that is symbolized by the black cross and the coming into flower symbolized by just one red rose. True enough, but the contrast between dying and coming into flower is enhanced if there is not just one rose—which is, of course, perfectly possible—but more than one. But why seven? If seven roses are included in the meditation, the most important thing is that they are a unified whole and not pieced together. Apart from that, the figure seven has a special quality of its own that is also apparent in some of the major time rhythms in evolution, and this serves to strengthen the effect of the meditation. It is merely a suggestion, however, and you are free to accept or reject; there is no rule about this. It is perfectly possible to have just one rose, but the effect will not be the same.

Another problem that some may experience is that the inner effort causes the muscles to tighten up and go into spasm. In that case the inner effort that was needed has gone in a direction that does not lead to creation of the image; it suddenly gets deflected. One can experience this as tension in the neck or another part of the body, or as grinding of the teeth.

This is best prevented by making sure that we are sitting in a relaxed upright position before we start and checking to make sure that this kind of tension does not develop anywhere in the body when the exercise starts.

Now come the third and fourth stages. Many people do not do these at all but only build up the image and meditate on it. That is perfectly all right, for the first two stages are valuable in their own right.

The third stage consists in making the image disappear and concentrating the attention on the inner powers that originally gave rise to it. This is usually far from easy, especially to begin with, and in most cases the result is absolutely nil. One then goes back to the first two stages and tries to intensify them. If sufficient intensity is achieved, we are more likely to succeed in extinguishing the image and concentrating the attention on the powers that had given rise to it. It will only be possible to live entirely in those powers for moments at a time. With practice and increased effort, however, it is possible to make those moments grow longer.

At the fourth stage, the powers that produced the image are also extinguished and all attention is focused on the spiritual entity that has given rise to those powers. As a rule, nothing at all will come to conscious awareness on which to focus meditative attention.

Once again it will be necessary to go back to the earlier stages and intensify the three stages of building up the image, living in the image and meditating on the image-producing powers. If we then go on to the fourth stage, often after practising for a very long time, we become conscious in our souls of the power that is the innermost core of our being.

A help in preparing for this most difficult fourth stage is the following.

Imagine the whole history of human evolution, spread before you as in a single vast canvas, and say to yourself that throughout the course of evolution no single individual has ever been able to do the Rose Cross Meditation. Having imagined this, let the idea arise that it is possible after all, but only on an entirely individual basis. To do this, the meditating individual needs to marshal that power of the spirit's innermost core. The next step is to focus our whole attention on that power, so that it will after all be possible to do the Rose Cross Meditation. This sequence of ideas can prepare us for the encounter with the true essence of our own higher self, which is the aim of the fourth stage.

The four stages of the Rose Cross Meditation may thus be summed up as follows:

Stage one   Building up the image in thought, entering into it with feelings, as deeply and intensely as possible. Our inner response to every conception is just as important as the thought content.

Stage two   Meditation on the image, entering wholly into it rather than merely contemplating it.

Stage three   The image disappears; concentration on the powers that created it.

Stage four   Encounter with the essential self; concentration on the spiritual entity that gave rise to the image-producing powers.

As already mentioned, it is certainly possible to stay with the first two stages, even for years if necessary. But we may be deceiving ourselves, for human individuals are generally capable of much more than they think; it is just that it is rather an effort to call up the necessary reserves of strength. We are also missing an opportunity if we never mobilize more than the powers that are immediately available and stop at the second stage. The very attempt—even if it fails—to venture on the third and fourth stages wakens powers in us that will intensify the first and second stages when we return to them. The powers we rouse in the effort pour into the work of building up the image and meditating on it. If the helpful suggestion given for the fourth stage is also taken up, so that attention is focused on the power of the spirit's innermost core, the building up of the meditation and the resulting image of the Rose Cross may be greatly enhanced as we now become aware of the nearness of our own higher self.

Thought Control

If we now leave the Rose Cross Meditation and look at everyday life, we soon realize that people often have great difficulty in achieving adequate concentration in thoughts and feelings. As soon as they begin to build up the meditation or enter into the actual process of meditation, they start to think of something entirely different. Lack of concentration is the problem. They cannot settle down to it, their thoughts flit around, scatter and jump from one association to another.

If this is the case, it is a good idea for them to return to everyday consciousness, but, rather than start with the first stage of the meditation again, do a preparatory exercise that will help to get their thoughts under control.

This exercise is not based on a major theme from human evolution but concentrates on a simple object—a penknife, for instance. All one does is to spend a short time, five minutes or so, on evolving thoughts on the penknife. It is important to take a very simple object, nothing complicated, but something perfectly ordinary and concentrate one's thoughts on it for five minutes, noting whether it is possible to stick to the subject for that period of time.

Every one of us has the powers that are needed to develop higher consciousness; it is merely that they lie dormant, that is to say, they are normally scattered, shooting off in all directions, so that we have no awareness of them. Thought control exercises concentrate those powers on a simple subject, where it is possible to hold them together. In this case, we ourselves decide what we are going to think about. In everyday life our thinking is governed mainly by the enormous variety of sensory perceptions; here, on the other hand, we have to exercise conscious control.

One might start with the knife blade, for instance. What is it made of, where did it come from and how was it produced? It is always important to stick with whatever we have decided to concentrate our thoughts on. It would be possible, for example, to think of just the tip of the blade for five minutes, but that would be rather more difficult, as there is less content to it. It is advisable, therefore, to start with something that has reasonable content and not make things too difficult to begin with. Later it may be possible to progress to a point where we concentrate on the tip of the blade only, which will require greater effort.

Our thoughts may of course also start to wander when we do this simple exercise with the penknife. Thinking of the material of which the blade is made, we may think of how the ores for the iron were produced from mines where veins of iron ores run below ground, etc., and before we know where we are we are thinking of the geological stages of the earth. Our thoughts have gone astray despite our staying on the subject, with the result that thought control has been lost. It is important to stick closely to the subject and determine exactly what is part of it and what is not, what takes us away from the object and what does not. The aim of the exercise is to increase our powers of concentration.

Please note that if the exercise is done only once the effect will immediately be submerged in all the uncontrolled thoughts that come to us throughout the day. The strengthening effect will only come when another important principle, the power of repetition, is brought to bear. If you decide to do the exercise not once but for five minutes every day for a month, the effect will be much greater; the ability to control your thoughts will be enhanced by the rhythmical element of repetition.

Something else that may happen is that when thought control has been practised a number of times one finds that the quality was much better at the beginning than at the tenth or eleventh time. You would assume that the more often you do an exercise the better the quality will be, but the reverse may well be the case. The reason is that concentration was at maximum pitch the first time, so that the exercise went well; it was new and interesting. This initial interest may be lost as time goes on and we tend to get careless, not keeping our thoughts firmly under control. Noticing this is, in fact, the first step towards dealing with the problem. It will be necessary to put more energy into the work now that the initial interest has gone. At this point another important principle begins to emerge: the exercises have to be done for their own sake; we must come to love them. The exercises must be done with love if they are to bear fruit.

It is interesting to consider how the thought control exercise relates to the Rose Cross Meditation.

There is no connection where content is concerned, but the power that has to be used to gain control is the same power that takes us to the fourth stage of the meditation. Without this power, which in thought control is in its germinal stage, we shall never achieve the final stage in the Rose Cross Meditation. It is well worth while to take careful note of the way in which the anthroposophical form of the meditative path is built up; the better we are at mastering this particular exercise the more intensive will be the way in which we are able to do the meditation.

The question also arises as to how much time should be spent on the Rose Cross Meditation and the thought control exercise, or on any meditation for that matter.

Initially, we ourselves decide how long it shall be, depending on the time available. In general it may be said, however, that a meditation of very short duration, half a minute or so, will have some effect, but not very much. The time may be extended until we have found our personal inner balance, for on the other hand there is also the danger of going on for too long. That is what happened to a young man, a follower of Rudolf Steiner, who tried to go through the night-time review exercise for a whole two hours and even then, going back through the day in reverse, only got as far as supper time. He mentioned this to Rudolf Steiner who told him that it was positively unhealthy to take so long over the review; the exercise could easily be done in a maximum of ten minutes. Rudolf Steiner suggested that the young man should do just a small portion of the review in painstaking detail and the rest in a single panoramic view. The small part done in detail would gradually increase and later on he would be able to do the whole review exercise in detail and only take five minutes.

The example shows that time management is an entirely down-to-earth, practical affair with meditations; that is to say, one attempts just as much as can be done in a reasonable time, while gradually seeking to increase the intensity.

Meditation on Personal Biography

Both the Rose Cross Meditation and the thought control exercise arouse powers in the soul that in anthroposophical circles are known as the faculty of Imagination. These image-forming powers go in a particular direction. They enable us to see life's events in images, gain living images of thoughts, be creative in shaping our thoughts, and so on. This may be represented by an arrow that points upwards (see page 20). When the meditation that has been described above—and others—has proved successful in this direction, we will initially feel great enthusiasm at the discovery of new powers gained and set out to increase our efforts in this direction with further meditations. There are many ways in which the effect can be strengthened, but these need not be gone into here; on the other hand a great danger also arises. Whenever meditations that lead to Imagination give results (this will, of course, only happen if considerable and sustained effort is made; sporadic exercises will not give results), there is the danger of becoming one-sided, of growing more egotistical without noticing it, of getting caught up in that new development, with our feet no longer quite on the ground.

In the preface to the third edition of his *Knowledge of the Higher Worlds: How is it Achieved?*, Rudolf Steiner put it like this:

'In this way it will be realized that the core of the matter does not lie in one truth, but in the harmony of them all. This must be very seriously borne in mind by those who wish to carry out the exercises. A particular exercise can be correctly understood and also correctly carried out; yet it can have a wrong effect if someone who is practising it does not add to it another exercise which resolves the one-sidedness of the first into a harmony of the soul.'*

This is shattering news—an exercise may be rightly understood and done and in spite of this have the wrong effect. But only if we do not add another exercise that will balance the one-sidedness of the first one and create harmony. What kind of exercise can create the necessary balance?

In the first place we must realize the importance of prior study, so that the path of knowledge is found in our thoughts. Every individual who meditates should ask: Where is the meditation I am reading or hearing about taking me? What kind of path is this, and how does it continue? Before we rush into doing any kind of exercise, we need to gain a clear understanding of the composition of the meditative path of knowledge as it is given in anthroposophy. (One may study the above book, or the chapter on 'Knowledge of Higher Worlds. Concerning Initiation' in Rudolf Steiner's *Occult Science: An Outline*.)

Below, details are given of what the next step should be, after doing exercises that take us in one direction, so that a harmonious balance may be established.

Rose Cross Meditation
Power to give form to thought

Biography Work
The light of consciousness in thought

The opposite direction that balances the Imagination exercises is primarily achieved by doing meditative work on one's own life. You start by asking yourself: What has the pattern of my day been from morning until night? What events did I come up against? Next: Where am I now in my

---

* Rudolf Steiner, *Knowledge of the Higher Worlds: How is it Achieved?* Rudolf Steiner Press, London, 1969. Preface to the third edition, p. 17.

life, my biography? How did I arrive at my present situation in the light of what has happened in recent years or since I was young?

All these questions have their origin with the inner observer that we mentioned in the first chapter (page 7). This observer is completely self-centred initially. We love ourselves most of all. This may go so far that the observer is always present in us and even interferes with our actions because of constant reflection on everything we happen to be doing. That is not what is meant here, however. It is rather a question of extending the role of the inner observer and directing it to our own past.

It is better not to start with your present situation, which would call for a high degree of objectivity, but with something that lies further back in time, say, in your eighteenth year. Bring to mind what went on in a particular situation then, something dramatic that may have had particular significance, possibly with a chaotic element to it, that had a powerful influence on you—something like that. The task is to recall this in every detail and at the same time look on it from a higher viewpoint, as if it had happened to someone else.

It is useful to remember that there is a tremendous difference between problems I experience in myself and those that someone else is going through. It is so much easier to be objective when it concerns someone else. It is therefore important to take an event that occurred some time ago and distance yourself from it, so that it can be considered objectively, from the outside, as it were.

Again, as with the Rose Cross Meditation, it is not the result that matters but the effort. The Rose Cross Meditation awakens dormant powers in us and the inner life is strengthened. The opposite is the case when we work with biography. The powers are already there—drives and passions and everything that is active in the will—and now this has to become conscious. The light of consciousness is directed on to an area where darkness normally reigns (see figure on page 20). To the power to give form to thinking activity and intensify feeling is now added the light of consciousness shed on the sphere of the will; just making the effort will achieve this.

That is the first stage in biography work, where the inner observer is made more powerful. This will not be done all day long, of course, but again only during a time chosen for the purpose, for ten minutes or so.

Once a certain mastery has been reached with this first stage, the next stage may follow; for this exercise, too, has a number of stages. The second stage is to distinguish the things that matter from those that do not matter. That is a definite step. If you merely make something objective and consider it, you do not yet differentiate between what matters and what does not.

This is something that cannot be immediately resolved; many people find it so difficult that they do not even try to get any further with it. 'How am I to judge what mattered and what did not—that would be nothing but a matter of subjective opinion!', they will say.

A number of things can resolve the issue; two of them are the following. In the first place you have to be clear that the question as to what matters and what does not has nothing to do with order of magnitude. Quite a minor event may have held much more significance than another one that at first sight seems to loom much larger in the biography. What matters is the extent to which the influence of an event goes beyond the given moment; something that initially seemed to be a powerful focal event in the biographic process may prove quite insignificant. Anything of passing significance is always of little significance. The things that matter are those that affect the biography as a whole, so that afterwards life has a slightly different colour.

The second thing is the question: Can I say that a particular event enhanced my powers of development so that I was able to progress? You may have had an illness and this may have involved thoughts and feelings that have since faded. It is possible, however, that by having to come to terms with the illness there may have been a change in disposition, in social attitudes or in character. I can therefore ask myself what carried more significance—the powers of development that caused me to progress inwardly, or all the thoughts and feelings, perhaps even the pain, that went with the illness? It is quite evident that the thoughts and feelings did soon pass, but the power of inner development cast its radiance into the life that followed.

Working with biography, we have to learn to take note of such significant aspects of development. We shall then also begin to be able to distinguish between what matters and what does not.

The stage of distinguishing between the essential and the inessential is followed by a further step that is of vital importance. Looking at a situation in life, when you were eighteen perhaps, and bringing it fully to mind, then trying to extract the significant aspects—which may not always succeed, but may gradually dawn on you—you suddenly come to realize that you were not alone in that situation; other people were there as well. In fact, nothing would have happened unless they had been there as well. You are now looking at your connection with other people and an image comes up that, to begin with, will be completely wrong. Why?

You see yourself at the centre of the event with the other people as smaller dots around you. You are the principal actor, the others are mere extras.

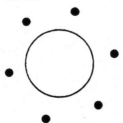

This overestimation of one's own importance is something we all share. It is a sickness that, in a way, is quite healthy for us; everybody has to go through it. We need this over-estimation initially so that we may achieve self-awareness and independence. It is always wrong, however, for without the other people we would not be what we are today. The sickness needs to be overcome, therefore.

Once we have become aware of this overestimation of self something can begin that I'd like to call 'rediscovering your fellow human beings'. We come to feel that unless this or that individual had played a particular role in a past event, none of it would have happened. Without that person I would not be the person I am today. A change occurs in the way I see things. The centre—me—grows smaller and smaller, and the periphery, the other people, grows in significance; they are no longer the extras I had thought them to be in my exaggerated estimation of self.

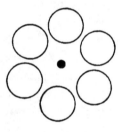

This may even go so far that the centre—me—disappears completely and the others become so much more real and important that I suddenly feel myself to be a mere nothing. Who am I to figure in this? Surely I am merely what others have made me, something brought together from many sources?

This is a crucial stage that has to be gone through with this meditation, but one that would be utterly wrong if taken by itself. I soon discover that I am still there at the centre—for it is indeed I who am making the judgement. Independent assessment has always to be done on an individual basis and cannot be done by someone else, otherwise it is just someone else's opinion. Our own power of judgement remains at the centre—and so does the capacity for love, for that, too, can only come from me and cannot be controlled from outside.

The next stage is to perceive the one-sided nature of the two different attitudes where either I am the only one who counts and the others are mere extras, or I am a mere nothing. I discover that I am not just there at the centre, I am also in the others; if I were not in them as well, I would not be at all. We are centre and periphery at one and the same time. Thus we discover a higher self that we may also call the true self, and this is deep inside us and also in those around us.

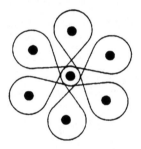

The direction our exercises take when we work with biography can be enhanced if we do not stick to one particular situation but gradually extend the meditation until it covers the whole of our life, right back to childhood. Biography work will then, bit by bit, create a whole panorama of life. Once again, it is best not to aim for this to begin with, but to start with a small part that can gradually be extended.

You may think your memory is not good enough for this, but you would be quite wrong. We have much greater ability to remember than we think, but we have to start with one little corner and then deepen it. Again it is the effort that counts, not the result.

This, then, balances the direction in which the Imagination exercises described in the first chapter take us. Practised on its own, Imagination would make us increasingly more egotistical, for it serves to strengthen the power to create inner images. To create a balance we must do biography work as well. Together with other exercises this meditation leads to what is known as Inspiration, a term that holds particular significance in this context. Inspiration in this sense has to do with everything that comes under the umbrella term of 'listening', listening to others.

Biography work improves our social skills, as it makes us aware of how we interact with others and of everything connected with our own biography.

It would of course be wrong to say that if image-producing meditation makes me more egotistical, then I'll skip it and go straight to biography work. If we did, we would not have the inner powers that we need to create the panorama of life; the result would be feeble and hollow, and it would get us nowhere.

It is necessary, therefore, to make that power really strong and then balance it with work on our own biography, so that social skills are enhanced. Each individual exercise is one-sided, but they balance each other.

It is like a breathing process. We have to take a good breath before we can exhale. The two are intimately bound up with each other and together produce the ebb and flow of our breathing.

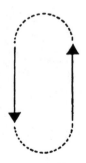

Practical Aspects

Some practical aspects of the exercises are the following. It is not a good idea simply to blunder one's way into a meditation, nor to have a tentative try at it. Care must be taken to be very deliberate in everything we do as we enter on a meditation. It is just like entering a room—we walk up to the door, open it and close it again behind us once we are inside. The same applies at the end of the meditation. When I finish, it is important to see that the meditation does not half unconsciously slip over into the rest of the day, so that I am still meditating a little when I am having my tea. Again the image of the door can be helpful. Leave the 'room' that you entered to do the meditation and close the door behind you as a sign that the meditation is over. You may certainly hold the mood of the meditation for a moment or two, but it is important not to let the contents of a meditation spill over into everyday life. A very deliberate approach to these matters is vital if development is to be harmonious.

As to the position of the body when meditating, it is best to sit upright for the Rose Cross Meditation, for the thought control exercise and for biography. It is bound to be more difficult to concentrate when lying down, which is easily found out by having a try. There are, however, meditations in which one tries to bring the moment of going to sleep and that of waking to full consciousness, and in this case one would obviously be lying down. The position of the body thus depends on the nature of the meditation. The same applies to other methods, such as the yoga method. With the latter, it would be necessary to go into the whole discipline in some detail before the different positions can be understood, but this book is clearly not the place for that. For the anthroposophical path the general principle is that we take our starting point in the life of soul and spirit, with thinking, feeling and will activity fully conscious. We usually sit upright during the meditation, with the body at rest and not disturbing the process, for that is what really matters.

As to the best time for doing a meditation, there are of course individual differences. Some people are freshest in the morning and then feel tired quite early at night; others need a long time to come really awake in the morning but are able to work well into the night. In spite of this, the time before one starts on the daily routine in the morning is generally a good one, and so is the late evening, when we can look back on what we have been doing in the course of the day. One can feel that these times offer spaces where it is easier to meditate than in the midst of the day and of work, for instance. Another good moment may be in the late afternoon. There can be no hard and fast rules about this and individuals need to find their own best time, possibly by trial and error.

With reference to the regularity of meditative work (see page 17) it should also be noted that a deepening occurs during the night that we may be aware of the next morning. If we stop doing the work, breaking the rhythm, a gap is created and there can be no further progress during the night that follows.

There may of course be occasions when we feel that we have not really understood a particular exercise. In that case we go back to the study stage and find out more about it. We then continue the work and try to establish a regular rhythm again.

It is always possible to intensify the work, but this is something that cannot be imposed from outside. The decision as to how much we are going to do has to be made in total freedom.

Interrupting a regular meditating rhythm will only prove harmful if the work has been so intense that spiritual organs have formed. An interruption would have an effect rather like being deprived of food, with the new organ no longer provided with the food it needs in the form of meditations. The organ would then wither away and we would be aware of this. In most cases the exercises are not so intense that actual organs are formed. That is part of a higher level of meditative work.

As for results, it is important, as already mentioned, not to build up false hopes. The results often come where one would least expect them. A lady who was a pupil of Rudolf Steiner had done the meditations to the best of her ability for seven years. She was a cultured lady and had achieved a high degree of personal freedom. Yet she had to confess to Rudolf Steiner that she was extremely worried about the results of her meditations. She told him that her studies in philosophy and anthroposophy were progressing well, which pleased her a great deal. But she was getting nowhere with her meditative work. Rudolf Steiner told her that she was utterly mistaken: if she had not faithfully done her meditations there would not have been the flowering that she had experienced in her other studies.

The effect of meditative work will as a rule show itself where we do not expect it. We meditate and then something happens in our life that otherwise would not have happened. Or something emerges during the night, while we are asleep, and we begin to wake up a little, without this affecting the physical body. The first beginnings of body-free conscious awareness begin to show themselves. Results will come, but usually in an area where we do not expect them, or in a different order of magnitude.

Meditation is always an entirely personal matter. We may talk to others about our own experiences, problems, etc., but it is pointless to meditate on a group basis if our own meditations are on the feeble side. Group meditation will not strengthen them. Strength can only be gained if we have done the work ourselves and then 'join forces' with others in a spiritual sense, by knowing that they are working with the same meditation. We are then working together at a higher level.

The same applies to having a teacher or guide. Personal

independence must be fully maintained if we ask anyone's advice. No one can do the work for us, but it is possible to seek advice and orientation from others who may be more advanced. The principle is to help people to help themselves.

One more comment on image-based meditation. It is of course also possible to meditate on a word or words, using the same technique to build up the meditation. In this case we do not use a visual image, but single words, phrases, or a mantra that create an auditory impression. The relationship of the one to the others is the same as that of eye to ear. There is of course an enormous difference between perceiving something with the eyes or with the ears, or between being blind, perhaps, or deaf. We experience the whole world of colour through our eyes and the world of sound with our ears, with our sense of speech and sense of thought. The two spheres combine in us, they complement each other but are entirely different in quality.

This is another instance where it is best to avoid one-sidedness and do both image- and word-based meditations. Each has its own intrinsic qualities and cannot take the place of the other. They enhance and enrich each other, but still make us one-sidedly egotistical unless balanced by biography work of the kind described above.

Will Control

Thought control is a definite help with the Rose Cross Meditation. Other exercises provide support for biography work. Many people do not find it easy to start a biographical review and may find it useful to do some preliminary exercises, two of which are described below.

These are 'will control' exercises. Paralysis of will is one of the major obstacles to biography work. You decide on a course of action and then fail to do it; you simply remain inactive and nothing else gets done. Another obstacle is a form of manic activity, when you are positively hyperactive from morning until night, getting drunk on your own activity; then suddenly the moment comes when there is nothing left to do, and you experience utter emptiness. Either extreme is a symptom of lack of independent will. An independent will bases itself on a clear decision made in a calm state of mind that is then carried out as planned.

There are, however, many people who do not even know this kind of will intent. They act only out of habit or a sense of duty, with no inner drive of their own, but only because it is what others expect. Such actions are of course a social necessity and not to be condemned. Yet it is also possible to do things that are not dictated from without, acting out of free personal initiative.

A simple exercise that helps in this direction is to decide to do something quite specific the following morning; for example: tie one's shoelaces not just once but twice—a small thing, quite insignificant in its outer aspect, that we have decided on. Night comes, and then the next morning, and the action is carried out.

It will often happen, however, that later on in the day we realize that we have simply forgotten to do that small thing. This is a strange experience, that comes not only to the careless but may indeed come to anyone at the beginning. Without noticing it, most of our actions are done on a routine basis of outer duties, strong habit, etc.

Will control helps us to do certain things entirely of our own accord. We then achieve a more objective relationship to ourselves, so that we find it easier to stand apart from ourselves and look at ourselves more objectively when we do biography work.

Another exercise is to deliberately change some of our habits. We all have certain peculiarities and characteristics, gestures and phrases we use that generally go back to child-hood, when we picked them up from our parents or teachers. The exercise involves taking note of such a peculiarity and trying to change it; we may for instance decide not to use a word that we tend to use rather frequently, and for a whole month use another word instead.

You would think that this is an easy thing to do, but it is not. Habits go deep, and we also experience an inner resistance, as if someone else were saying: 'I don't want to change; I'll stay as I am.' This resistance has to be overcome.

We may also find, however, that we are able to change after all and that it is possible to shape the substance of our lives. This then becomes a minor source of strength, a help in working with our own biographies.

The less we are in control and the less light is brought into the darkness of the will sphere, the less will we be able to have an overview of our biographies.

This takes us into everything connected with shaping our own lives, a sphere in which we can gradually come to perceive more and more clearly that we are following a path of inner development. However imperfect this path may be, it leads to our own higher self and as we work on our biographies we begin to discover that self.

The Path to the Higher Self

Everything done so far has served to bring dormant powers to life in us (first chapter) and made us take a new look at our biographies (second chapter). We had thought our ego consciousness to be much more important than anything in the world around us; now we have to make the discovery that everything on the periphery of our life is in fact part of ourselves, that the small ego consciousness at the centre can expand to include other individuals with whom we have a connection. Another, higher self can be dimly sensed; we do not perceive it clearly but realize that it is something great and all-inclusive. It is possible to sense that one's own power of development is somehow connected with the relationship between small ego consciousness and large periphery.

The question arises as to where the power of development has its origin. Looking back on life, as far as we are able, and reviewing it, we then ask ourselves: When was the power that carried development forward at its peak? The answer is clear—in every individual this power is greatest during the first three years of life. As a rule, we are unable to remember that time in our lives, but if we consider what goes on in a child during those first three years, we realize that giant steps are taken in development at a time when there is as yet no conscious reflection and no ego consciousness.

Infants reach a stage when they stand upright and begin to walk; if they did not do so they would have to crawl for the rest of their lives and the potential for development would be extremely limited. The upright position offers fundamental developmental potential for the whole biography, and the power that achieves this step in development is the one that is later used in the Rose Cross Meditation—the power of the developing human being. It is used unconsciously in early childhood, though even then it is a form of exercise; think of

how many times children must make the effort until they are
finally able to stand—rather wobbly at first, but then more and
more securely—and finally also to walk. They radiate joy
when they have finally mastered the art.

The same applies to learning to speak and to think. These,
too, are giant steps in development that provide the basis for
everything that follows.

The tremendous power of development that infants have
can be compared with what adults are able to experience
when ego consciousness is fully developed. Rudolf Steiner has
presented interesting discoveries relating to this, which are
quoted below.

'We thus see that man accomplishes momentous things
during the first years of his life. He is working on himself in
the spirit of the highest wisdom. In point of fact, if it were a
question of his own cleverness, he would not be able to
accomplish what he must accomplish without that cleverness
during the first period of his life. Why is all this accomplished
in those depths of the soul which lie outside consciousness?
This happens because the human soul and entire being are,
during the first years of earthly life, in much closer connection
with the spiritual worlds of the higher hierarchies than they
are later... Whereas what we call the child's aura hovers
around it during its earliest years like a wonderful human and
superhuman power and, being really the higher part of the
child, is continued on into the spiritual world, at the moment
to which memory goes back, this aura sinks more into the
inner being of the child... This is not the case with a very
young child, to whom things appear only as a surrounding
world of dreams. Man works on himself by means of a wisdom which is not within him. That wisdom is mightier and
more comprehensive than any conscious wisdom of later
years. The higher wisdom becomes obscured in the human
soul which, in exchange, receives consciousness...

'What is present in childhood to a supreme degree, so that
the individual is then working out of a self which is still in

direct connection with higher worlds, continues to some extent even in later years, although the conditions change in the manner indicated above.'*

We have thus gained ego consciousness at the cost of losing contact with the world of the spirit. This does not mean, however, that the spiritual powers of development cease completely. A small, unnoticed trickle continues, though it is nothing like the powerful stream of the first three years of life. Where are these powers to be found in adult life?

We find them in adults when they do not stand still and stagnate, but say to themselves: I cannot go on like this, for the way I am now I am nothing but a caricature of myself. At this point adults are, metaphorically speaking, coming upright and beginning to walk—on the strength of those powers of development. It is possible to take oneself by the scruff of the neck and come awake, and this shows that the source of developmental powers has not dried up. There are all kinds of other evidence of this as well.

The human physical body has a power that may be called the 'power to heal itself'. This shows itself when minor wounds heal of their own accord, requiring no medical treatment. It really is a minor miracle: a small wound has simply disappeared after a while, leaving no trace. It is the wholeness of the human being, the vital whole of the body, that restores a minor injury and makes the tissues part of the whole again. Illness always means that part of the body has dropped out of context, and healing consists in restoring it to that context. Healing could never occur if it were not for this power of self-healing.

Individuals differ in the degree to which they have this inherent power. The same power is active here that works in a young child, in adults who achieve moral uprightness, and in the meditation that is part of the path of development. These

---

*Rudolf Steiner, *The Spiritual Guidance of Man*. Anthroposophic Press, New York, 1976. Lecture One.

are different aspects of the developing human being.

We are now gradually approaching the reality of the higher self. The higher powers in us lose potency as ego consciousness develops. We cannot do without that ego consciousness, however, for it is the basis of independent judgement and free will.

The question arises as to how we can retain ego consciousness and at the same time establish a new connection with the higher powers that were so tremendously effective in our early years. It is a question of how to find the way to our higher self. There is no egotism in this, for the higher self is not limited to the individual but lives just as much in the periphery—as we may come to know in our biography work. That periphery goes beyond the immediate social sphere, however, and we gradually discover that we are connected with the whole of humanity and with the physical world, being unable to live without the one just as much as without the other. The higher self lives in my limited ego consciousness and at the same time also in the vast periphery of my life.

We can gain increased awareness of our connection with the physical world by becoming aware of the fact that our character would have quite a different complexion if we had grown up in a village high up in the mountains rather than in a large city. The whole sphere of sensory experience is totally different if the murmuring forests, the meadows and brooks of mountain country formed the background to one's childhood, or else the roar of traffic, the lights of the big city and the street canyons between high-rise buildings. Those impressions have made each of us what we are just as much as the people who have been around us. We are thus able to become aware of our relationship to the world, a relationship based on sensory impressions. We come to realize that the sphere of sensory experience is part of the path to the higher self and the more effort we put into this sphere, the more will we be able to know the higher self.

Positivity Exercise

When we begin to be more aware of what goes on in the sphere of sensory perception we soon realize how superficial our sensory perceptions usually are. We find that we hardly ever show genuine interest in the physical world or in the people around us. If I do take a closer interest in certain objects or people this is often only out of a one-sided ego-tistical desire to possess them, because I feel that they are important to me. This kind of egotistical sympathy is not a real relationship to my environment, nor is the one-sided rejec-tion and antipathy that does not even allow me to perceive what someone else or some physical object has to offer.

This is a situation we all know, for none of us is free from egotism, but it can be overcome with the 'positivity exercise'.

The thought and will control exercises described above serve to enhance the inner potential we have—the one in our thinking, the other in our will. The positivity exercise is used to enhance our relationship to the outside world, that is to say, to other people and to the physical world around us.

At first sight, positivity might be taken to mean that one simply grants others the right to be as they are. Yet while it is certainly part of the exercise not to think or talk negatively about others, this does not mean that we should simply overlook negative aspects. There is a great deal more than this to the exercise. On the one hand it is important to see the shadow side, and on the other to discover the positive side, even if we are fully aware of the faults. I cannot call myself truly positive unless I have discovered something completely new and positive in the other that I did not know before. It is in making that discovery that I increase my perceptiveness and perhaps come a little more awake.

That is only the first step, however, and there is more to come. I can make the new discovery an inward experience and enter into it with my feelings; this will lead to the dis-covery of further positive aspects. By making positivity an inward experience I enhance my powers of perception and my interest in the other individual.

If our relationship with someone else has been extremely negative and we have then come to discover something in them that is truly positive, we find that we discover even more that is positive at the second stage. A kind of 'breathing process' develops: first we enter more strongly into perception, reaching out to discover something new and making it an inward experience; then we go outwards again, having increased our powers, and discover more that is new.

Initially this can be practised in our relationships with people, but the same process also applies to all the sensory impressions we gain from the physical world—colours, sounds, etc. We discover that we have not really taken them in until now. We usually pass by the objects, let them be what they are and really are not at all interested. We shut ourselves off so that we won't be overwhelmed by a flood of impressions. The positivity exercise overcomes this; we discover new things and our perceptions are intensified—this flower, that tree, a particular colour, and every new discovery that becomes part of inward experience creates the ability to take in more that is new. The relationship to the world around us is enhanced and we come to realize that we are intimately bound up with it. This is one way of finding our own higher self, which is part of the world around us just as much as it is part of ourselves.

Acquired Idealism

The path to the outside world has to be complemented by that of inner strength. Two paths lead to the higher self. Each may be taken on its own initially, but only for a short distance, for all impetus is lost unless the other path is taken as well.

The positivity exercise is the path to the outside world; the world we perceive, other people and the physical world are taken very seriously and brought to inward experience, so that perceptiveness and our interest in the world are enhanced. The other path is one that we take within ourselves, independent of the outside world. We may call it the path of idealism.

There is genuine and false positivity and there is also genuine and false idealism. A positivity that is not genuine finds everything equally good and lets people and things be as they are without taking a real interest in them. Idealism that is not genuine involves having ideas and ideals as to how the world ought to be, what I ought to be and—above all—what other people ought to be. It is easy to wax enthusiastic over such ideals without doing any inner work. I am fired by ideals but do not take a single step to change the way I am.

This kind of 'flash-in-the-pan' idealism flares up but does not lead to anything. It is particularly common in young people. They have not made the least effort to achieve it and profess lofty ideals without having brought anything to realization in themselves. It could also be called 'congenital' idealism. If it is the only kind of idealism we have, need will arise for a completely new kind of idealism—one that is acquired, which calls for effort and for overcoming of self, an idealism that takes me beyond myself and wants to become active within me. I have great ideals before me, but they are there to help me to develop and go beyond what I have become so far.

Flash-in-the-pan idealism is always lacking in modesty and generally demands that others should change. Acquired idealism is modest, for it can only be brought to realization slowly and demands that I, myself, change. Flash-in-the-pan idealism does not take us forward on the meditative path; we fire up with enthusiasm for higher knowledge but in reality nothing happens at all.

The true path to knowledge demands that we grow beyond ourselves, perceive ourselves as we are, distance ourselves from that perception and add something new. The same gesture is to be found in the Rose Cross Meditation that has been described in the first chapter. The image of the black cross includes me, myself, and everything in me that must die and be overcome. The red roses coming into flower on the other hand hold within them what I make of myself, beyond what I have been so far.

The Rose Cross Meditation as an image of human development can become more than an image; we can reach a point where it becomes a concrete, living reality.

Acquired idealism makes us take an objective view of ourselves, letting some things go and others come into flower instead, or transforming the old into something new. We always have areas in us that can be transformed and also things that should be let go. Something old therefore dies to make room for new growth.

The two paths are complementary, one being the path of positivity, called the 'thought path' by Rudolf Steiner, the other the path of acquired idealism, Rudolf Steiner's 'will path'. Both take us to experiences that will be discussed in the next chapter. (See also the lecture Rudolf Steiner gave in Zurich on 11 February 1919, in *The Inner Aspect of the Social Question.*★)

Initially either path may be taken on its own—inner development or acquired idealism. However, if we fail to take account of other people when taking the second path, there is a danger of growing poor in mind and spirit as well as in our humanity because we have not developed the positive approach that is also needed.

If we take only the path that takes us outside ourselves, practising positivity but failing to grow ourselves, we soon lose impetus and come to a halt, for we lack the power to take hindrances, obstacles and set-backs and make them into something positive. The inner strength that is gained must

---

★ Rudolf Steiner Press, London, 1974.

serve the environment, and the process must also work in the other direction.

We can see an analogy to this in early childhood development. Children first come upright and do so entirely out of their own resources—that is the inner aspect. They then begin to talk. If they did not turn to the outside world they would never learn to talk. They have to relate fully to that world and listen to other people talking if they are to acquire language skills.

Both directions are unconsciously taken in early childhood, and they continue to be effective when adults set out on the meditative path of knowledge, for then the powers of childhood development continue to act in a new and metamorphosed way.

The Encounter with Christ

If we take a look at history to see for how long human beings have been able to take the path of inner development, it is fair to say that the path could certainly have been followed 200 or so years ago. The potential was also there during the Middle Ages, though no doubt in a slightly different way. Yet as soon as we go back to pre-Christian times we note a fundamental difference. The powers of childhood development and their metamorphosed form for use in initiation clearly existed also during the ancient Greek, Egyptian and other advanced civilizations, but they came from outside, that is, from the social environment of the group, tribe or nation. Until the time of ancient Greek civilization, individuals were supported by their social environment. Little importance attached then to the ability to judge for oneself. The collective consciousness of the tribe into which individuals were born determined the actions of the individual. We may thus say that the powers of development were given to individuals from the environment; they were not inherent in the individual. Admission to the mystery centres was regulated by the chief priests who acted in the collective tribal interest; it was not determined by the seeking individual. In the mystery centres, the aim was first of all to eradicate individual self-awareness, so that the individual could be made into an instrument or organ for the tribe or nation. At that time, the powers of development did not yet act through the eye of the needle that the individual ego represents.

We find no evidence of individual powers of development until we come to Socrates who spoke of them and also clearly possessed them. There are however crucial moments in his dialogues where he would still speak of the super-individual power of the 'demon' (see Plato's *Apology* 31c f. and *Phaedrus* 242a f.).

Comparison of documents from the pre-Christian and Christian eras shows that a decisive change had occurred, and this has to do with the great Christian impulse.

At the beginning of the Christian era came the event of which John wrote in the prologue to his Gospel that the Word, who was in the beginning and through whom all things were made, had become flesh and dwelt among us. Today the power of that Word, the power through which all that is has come into being, is in every human individual. From now on the World Word is active in every human being, with the pendulum swinging to and fro between inside and outside, as described above.

When we look up to the divine creator, the ground and origin of the whole world, we perceive the divine principle as God the Father. The Father lives and works as the source and origin of all that is in the world, but he does not become concentrated and individualized and as such enter into individual human beings. That, however, is the key element in the Christ event. The creative Word (Logos), out of whom all that is has come, entered into one particular human being at the baptism in the river Jordan; that individual then became Jesus Christ, 'Son' of God and at the same time also 'Son of Man'. Having gone through His passion and death on the cross, the risen Christ became the power of development that is active in humanity as a whole and in every individual human being, the power of real love that can engender overcoming of self, power of sacrifice and understanding for other human beings and for everything there is in the world. Christ Himself is the potential for development that exists in every human being and in humanity as a whole.

He was also present in pre-Christian times, as was known in the ancient mysteries, but His influence then came from outside. In those times people had to look outside themselves for guidance to higher development; they were supported by external powers that had not yet become individual. Then came the great reversal; since then, Christ enters into the individual human ego—if the individual is a Christ seeker. He does not come unasked. Paul used the following words to describe this: 'Not I, but Christ lives in me.'

It is now possible to give a more precise definition of the two paths described in the third chapter—the path of positivity, which is inward, and the path of acquired idealism, which goes outward.

If I were to say, 'I can find Christ within me; I do not need other people,' I would be in error. We can find Christ in us, but only if we also find Him in the other person. What happens if individuals look for Christ only in themselves and take no interest in the reality that lives in another person? This tendency is apparent in numerous religious experiences that are also called 'Christ experiences'. Something that originally may well have genuinely come to life in one's heart does not manage to come to life also in real encounters with other human beings, so that one perceives Christ in the other person; instead there is an experience of inner joy that has a definitely egotistical element to it.

There are two ways and both lead to Christ—in the other person and in the power to develop our own life. The two act together to become one way, and only then do they become true.

The initial experience, here described entirely at the level of thought, can be taken forward in a number of steps.

First there is the possibility of coming closer to Christ in understanding. Step by step we take in the *Christ idea*, the way it has come to realization in history and in individual people. This may gradually become less hazy and more clearly defined and will then be transformed into something that I'd like to call the '*Christ impulse*'. At this point the idea becomes reality, it is no longer merely a thought. The third and final step is the '*Christ encounter*'; it comes when the impulse has become increasingly active.

The Christ idea may be extremely nebulous to begin with, for we encompass it only in our thoughts. We perceive it to be a great and all-encompassing idea, but it will continue to be rather tenuous for quite a long time. There is nothing wrong with this; on the contrary, it is a good thing for understanding to dawn slowly, remaining entirely open to whatever may follow.

The next step calls for increased personal initiative, for it is this which changes idea into impulse. Personal initiative is a precondition in the effort to gain understanding. Initially there may be a long time when our understanding has no real effect on our life; it appears to remain in the background. Yet true understanding is also the budding impulse, for it wants to come to full realization. Such will-imbued understanding is then an existential issue; it does not, however, come of its own accord but can only be achieved through increased personal initiative.

That initiative has to follow the pendulum swing that has already been referred to—moving inwards to enhance the powers of personal development and then outwards so that we enter fully into other people. Now the Christ impulse begins to come to experience in our thoughts and feelings and in the will, but to begin with it is rather general—not tenuous, but general. It is a power of the spirit that we know extremely well but it is still rather general.

'General' in this context means the following. I may be sitting by myself and thinking of the whole of humanity. That is 'general'. My thoughts become more concrete if I think of individual people whom I know. They are somewhere else, however, far away, perhaps in another country. Now the door may open and a friend comes in and I talk to him. I can now compare this third stage with the first. When I think of humanity as a whole, this is something entirely at the thought level; it is general but with the whole of humanity present in it. The general element is thus wholly in my thoughts, which of course does not make it unimportant. I then progress from the general to the particular, which is the opposite direction to that taken in modern science. There one starts with the observation of details and arrives at generally applicable laws. In the science of the spirit we start from the general and slowly come to the particular. Thus the whole of humanity was initially present in my thoughts, and a concrete encounter was not possible; then my friend came in and we were able to meet, person to person.

The same applies to our relationship with Christ. The Christ idea may be in our minds all our life, and that is perfectly justifiable. The idea may also condense into the Christ impulse, though this may remain rather general for a long time. Again there is nothing wrong with this, for the whole of me has to be able to grow with this slow process of condensation. Then comes the stage of the direct encounter, as when we meet a friend.

Christ will not be perceived in the physical human form that lived almost two thousand years ago as Jesus of Nazareth. Nevertheless, Christ is a concrete presence in this encounter, just like the friend who visits me in person. The experience leaves the definite impression that I experience Christ because He sees me—that is, His eyes behold me—and I am able to share consciously in the experience. He then lives in me.

If one merely has a vision of what seems like a physical form, perhaps a figure of light, this is either something entirely different or it is a preparatory stage to being seen by Christ. The Christ encounter occurs purely in soul and spirit, where essence meets essence, but the degree of condensation is such that it appears to be on the very edge of physical, sensory perception, at a particular moment and on a particular day.

The nature of the encounter differs from individual to individual. As a rule, however, it only takes place when the individual faces enormous difficulties and has to go through a zero point. In the Rose Cross Meditation the black cross marks a threshold point, and in a similar way we may reach a point of absolute nothingness in life, a moment of death when nothing seems to be able to take us onward. When we have come to the limit of despair and of total impotence, a point where we'd simply like to give up and put an end to our own life—if we are able to bear this and try to penetrate beyond it, then it may happen that Christ is suddenly there, as a friend, immediately perceptible at the moment. Angelus Silesius wrote:

> Unless it raiséd be in thee,
> the cross on Golgotha
> cannot from evil powers
> thy saviour be.

Many people have spoken of this moment of encounter that has often come in times of extreme need, in war, etc. Yet again it is only a beginning. If we were to think that we have now achieved the highest goal, the greatest bliss attainable, we would no doubt be in error. It has to be seen as the beginning of a new way; otherwise it will simply fade away.

A crucial question connected with the Christ encounter is whether it can only be achieved by years of meditative effort, going through every single stage—Rose Cross Meditation, thought control, biography work, etc. That is not the case. The encounter may come at any moment, quite unexpectedly, and to anyone, even if they have not been meditating. The question is how does the encounter with Christ relate to the meditative path to knowledge?

The encounter cannot be forced, just as I cannot force a friend to visit me. It lies in the initiative of Christ whether or not He comes to visit me. The encounter is a grace that is given to me. It can also happen to several people at the same time, for Christ is so all-encompassing that He can appear to one person and another at one and the same time.

Anyone who has made intense efforts to follow the meditative path to knowledge, both inward and outward, will be prepared for the moment of that encounter in the spirit. The meditative way helps our understanding and enables us to do further work on this source. Before, we have only been dimly aware of the power of development within us, the power that is active in young children, in every meditation, and which can also be experienced in our relationships to others when we do biography work and when we go outward in the positivity exercise. Now it becomes a real entity. We are familiar with the quality and know immediately what it is, so that we do not feel tempted to dwell in happiness and rest on our laurels. We can only prepare for the encounter, however; we cannot bring it about.

An event like this, which anyone may experience from about the eighteenth year onwards, continues to be with us for the rest of our life. It does not become more distant as time goes on, but is always there, if we call it to mind. Time becomes space in our minds, so that this past event always remains in the immediate present and constantly lends new strength to the shaping of our own life.

Is it possible to ask oneself at any time: 'Have I strayed from the path?' The potential to go astray is always there. If we become too self-centred and deviate from the truth we sense that the Christ experience grows shadowy and withdraws slightly from consciousness. It never goes completely, but the error of our ways draws a veil before it. The experience therefore needs to be sought anew in every practical life situation of the moment.

This, then, outlines the area of Christ experience, as far as is possible in the given situation.

The aim of this book has been to show the relationship between the meditative anthroposophical path of knowledge and experiences of the nearness of Christ. If we truly desire this nearness of Christ, it will accompany the path of knowledge at every one of the stages described.